Nothingness: Love Poems

Bharat Luthra

Nothingness is a collection of epistolary love poems. It is a lover's soul in wonder at love. It is love in its rawest form.

Author:

Bharat Luthra (Bharat Bhushan) better known as Leaf is a thinker and writer. He runs a foundation dedicated to advocacy for centralized global governance rooted in Civitology and the mitigation of climate change. He believes that the purpose of human civilization is to grow as old as possible, a goal that can only be pursued through unity, collective righteousness, and individual righteousness.

He is the originator and father of ***Civitology**, science of civilizational longevity*. He is working to establish Civitology as a scientific discipline to ensure the sustainability, peace, and long-term survival of human civilization. His book on Civitology is scheduled for release soon.

ISBN-13: 978-933-430-992-8
ISBN-10: 933430992X

Published by: Bharat Bhushan
Edition: Second (Revised) Edition, 2025

Note to the Reader:
The poems in this collection delve into emotional and existential extremes, including devotion, intimacy, loss, despair, and mortality. Certain passages contain explicit language and imagery. This book is intended for mature readers.

BharatLuthra.com
OnenessJournal.blogspot.com
Instagram.com/BharatPoetry

TABLE OF CONTENTS:

Desire

Before the Big Bang,
before the circumstances,
which would lead
to the so believed Big Bang,
before the beginning of everything,
there was nothing.
Cosmologists,
quantum physicists, and astrophysicists
go on piercing numerous equations
to their furthest roots
to puzzle out
the origins of existence.

They go on analysing
the state of the universe
with thermodynamic laws
and the chemical formation
of every new element
they get their hands on.

But there is a metaphysical
theory to it,
and in that,
I want to talk about a state
when even time did not exist,
when there was not a
single fleck of matter,
or antimatter, or any energy.

There was no sound,
not even silence,
neither chaos nor stillness,

neither light
nor darkness,
and not even
the singular point
from which the Big Bang
is considered to have taken off.

Essentially,
there was nothing.

But something prevailed
in that nothingness.

And the scientists
do not have
any explanations
for the presence of that thing,
or any formulas to quantify it,
nor any laws
that would explain its nature,
and will never have
those laws
or formulas either.

That most elementary something
is desire.

All manifestation,
unlike what they tell you,
is not the outcome of randomness,
but it was desired.

And the state of nothingness
was brimming,
terribly brimming with such desire.

It desired substance.
It desired energy.
It desired both light and dark.
It desired life.
It desired purpose.

It desired all the things
which would give meaning to it.

And it began.

Nothingness started to make love to itself.
It started to make love to her desire.
It started to procreate with itself.
It started to procreate with her desire,
and all of it led to creation.

That desire gave birth to everything,
starting from the formation
of the simplest
of all the elements,
which further broke down
into other complex forms.

And those forms,
again accumulating
and breaking into each other,
formed more and more elements
along the way,
together with their endless evolution,
which will go on
for an endless time.

From the very first cell
to every living thing,
desire gave birth to all.

Desire is the root
of each emotion,
which springs in the human heart,
and the human soul,
be it love,
joy,
or suffering.

Desire wounds.
Desire heals.
Desire cages.
Desire sets free.

And desire is,
has been,
and shall remain
the mother
of every creation.

And, my love,
you are that desire,

that mother.

Like a Star

There is a certain aura
that she scatters
around her
just with her presence,
like a star
firing light
from its cannon,
breathtaking,
and unstoppable.

Fire and Water

She is both
fire and water,
something that burns you
yet you can not live without.

Prison

She is the kind of prison
that will make you
lock yourself in
and then eat the keys.

Unrequited Love

Allow me to teach you
the suffering of unrequited love.
It is like continuously building
the new chambers of hell
inside your heart,
and silently hoping
your beloved
ceases that construction.

Delusions in Love

Delusions in love
are like this;

you enter her heart
and feel at home.
Everything looks
the way you imagined,
like it is your own,
your destined place.

But then she tells you
that it does not need
anyone.

And you think,
this heart has
waited for you
for eons.
Now is the time
you arrived.
And if it needs
someone,
it has to be you.
So you try to stay.

But then she tells you
that it belongs to
someone else.

And you think,
maybe that person is you,
and she is just playing

a mushy game
that you have
to win.
And you want to stay.

But then she tells you
it does not belong to you,
but to someone else.

And you think,
maybe you should wait.
For it is your own home.
It must invite you back.
So you wait
until it is vacant again.

Once vacated,
you enter again,
prancing like its sole possessor.
But she tells you to get the fuck out,
closing the door on you,
for it does not need anyone,
and certainly not you.

And you think,
you are an impatient fool,
and you should have waited
some more.
Maybe it was not
the right time.

So you pass a little time
until the heart falls into place.
Then you trespass

the closed door,
and she again pushes you out.

And while standing outside,
you think of the gentleness
of that push,
naming it silent care,
a love that could be kindled.
And you build hope on it.

With that little hope,
you trespass again,
without hustling,
without making any sound,
like a soldier
who has come
to reclaim his own state.

But you see
all the demons and angels
of the heart
coming together,
carrying their broadswords,
crying out for your blood.

They catch you
and beat the love
and hope out of you.
You are almost
beaten to death,
and then dragged
outside the heart.

Gravely injured,
barely conscious,

with blood dripping
from places
you never imagined,
you lie outside
the heart.

And you think
that something is wrong
with the heart,
your home,
your destined place,
and that only you
could mend it.

Pieces

You never wanted me as a whole,
so I give you myself in pieces,

and I will continue to
sprinkle myself over you
until you have realised
that each of these pieces
was made for you.

Two Atoms

If not in this life,
we will meet some other time,

maybe countless years from now.
Maybe not as whole as we are now,
but as small as single atoms.

At that time,
I can imagine
a single atom of mine,
carrying all my love,
dashing into an atom of yours.

But just how cruel
would this universe be
if it does not let
even that happen?

And while I say this,
the madman inside me
invents a more glorious story
than this,

a story of two atoms,
that we are made up of,
which have longed to collide
for countless years
until this life.

MADMAN

All her lovers have tried
to understand her,
like scholars
of a sacred subject.

They try to study her
as she is,
as she has been,
and as she might be;
from the things she does,
has done,
does not do,
and may do.

They enter her
from the softest corners
and crawl their way
to the five-layered heart.

First layer pierced.
In this layer,
they learn about the things
and the places
that make her happy.

Second layer pierced.
In this layer,
they study her scars
and the things that make her sad,
so they can keep her away from those things.

Third layer pierced.
This layer accounts for the trust

that she must have in you
to let you through it,
and that is it.

She would not allow anyone further,
not even the scholars she loves
and made love to.

No one can reach the fourth layer,
let alone touch it.

And the fifth layer,
I am forbidden
to write about that,
because she herself
has no clue about it yet.

And I keep telling the scholars,
the layers of her heart
are a lethal labyrinth,
and they are going to lose everything
by the time they reach the third layer,
because there is no backing out.

But simultaneously,
I ask them not to lose hope,
for there is a reward waiting for them,
a reward bigger than anything
they can think of.

Beyond that layer
lies something more
than this universe has to offer.

So I ask them
not to give up.
Stretch your hands.

Keep reaching for the layer.
Keep crashing yourself into it.
Maybe you will get a nod
for the most precious elements
of this multiverse.

By now,
you may be wondering,
who am I,
and how do I know
the intricacies of the layers of her heart
to this magnitude?

Well, I am just another scholar
who was prohibited from studying her.
I am an autodidactic correspondent
who may have mastered
studying her from a distance.

I am the madman
you would have seen outside temples,
mosques, gurdwaras,
and churches on Sundays,
in a tattered shirt and pyjamas,
with a shabby beard
smeared with leftover food
he was given
but could not eat,
because he was too obsessed with her.

I am the madman,
who keeps talking to himself
about illusory theories
about love
and the non-biological layers of the heart,

immersed in his soliloquies,
which you can not comprehend
from the gurgling sounds
falling from his mouth,
except for being scared
and feeling equally blessed
as you turn around,
for not having a destiny like his.

Your Hands

This universe
can not collect all my broken pieces
in my entire lifetime
to build me as a whole again,
but you could,
that too with
a single firm embrace.

For me,
your hands hold more magic
than the universe
cosmologists spend their whole lives
wondering about.

Throat

I am a throat
parched for the eternities
that has recklessly believed you,
and just you,
to be the only water body
present in this universe.

Mystic Hole

It is as if
there is a hole in me,
which could suck
the entire universe into it,
and maybe just your love
would suffice
to fill it to the brim.

Wanderers

Had you been my girlfriend,
I would have taken both of us
to the remotest riparian forest
in the world,
far away from humans,
where we could not be traced
for the rest of our lives.

Once we made it there,
it would begin,
the journey of two wanderers:

The jungle,
breathing raw
and primal life,
melodies of birds whispering
the entire evolution into our ears,
the scent of trees cleansing our lungs,
and sacred soil
seeping the pulse of Mother Earth
into our bodies through our bare feet,

There would be no other art
except nature
and the art we would make.

Some days we would remain naked,
as naked as we were born,
using herbs over our bodies
to protect ourselves from insects,
living off plants and river water,
we would make a small house

with straw and bamboo
and decorate it with
everything crafted by our own hands.

We might have our own band.
You would do the rap,
and I would do the beatbox.
We would dance
and make a lot of music,
a lot of poetry,
and even a lot of love,
if you wished.

We would laugh.
We would cry.
We would make many memories.

We would be there for each other
every moment,
like the shore is there for the ocean,
and the ocean for the moon,
and the moon for the Earth,
and the Earth for the sun,
and vice versa.

Mother Nature's truthful mornings,
and her stark nights,
where the sun and the moon
would undress themselves along with us,
and the stars would shine more gloriously.

All of her seasons would be real,
more real than we have known them so far.
Her rain would pour like music,
and we would let Mother Nature

consume us with her raw beauty
and unveil her secrets and truths to us,
which we could not learn otherwise.

And maybe we would return
to human civilization someday,
rejuvenated,
reborn,
having learned and unlearned ourselves,
burning with many stories
to share with the world,
and burning with yet another adventure.

Heart and Arms

This body of mine has a heart
that has grown cold
from being vulnerable for too long,
but it still has those arms,
which, when wrapped around,
can build the warmest
and safest home
you will ever find.

Drug of Love

I want you to think of me
whenever you look at a tree,
or gaze at the moon,
or bathe in the sun,
or see yourself in a mirror.

I want you to think of me
whenever you listen to a song,
or read a poem,
or draw a doodle,
or touch yourself.

I want your hands
to remind you of mine,
and your bosoms,
your hair,
and your body scent.

I want you to think of me
whenever it rains,
each drop carrying my presence
and collapsing it
over your skin.

I want you to think of me
whenever you go to bed,
before you fall asleep,
and in your dreams,
and whenever you wake up,
to be the first thought
in your mind.

I want you to think of me
during work breaks,
and while you work,
during moments of idleness,
during hectic schedules,
and over tight deadlines.

I want you to look for me
in known faces,
and in strangers,
in every picture,
and in each abstraction.

Think of me,
my eyes,
my hair,
my face,
my voice,
how I walk,
how I am typing away in a room,
unceasingly thinking about you,
the same way I ask you
to think of me.

And now, with these words,
I wonder if I can ignite you
with the same drug of love
which I am always high on.

But I know
this would not work unless
you have tasted love
like I have,
or you could replace
the machine pounding inside my chest

with the one
that pounds inside yours.

Knowing You

If a young man
loses his eyesight,
he is going to suffer a lot more
than a man who was born blind,
because the young man
had seen and lived the beauty
that colors possess.

And, my love,
the same thing will happen
to every person
who will have to live without you
after knowing you.

Mystic Lock

The door to her heart
had a mystic lock,
aesthetic, sturdy,
and with as many combinations
as the number of atoms in the universe;
a lock of its only kind,
made of a pattern
that could form only once
in eternity.

And all the gods,
all the kings,
all the queens,
all the devils,
all her comrades
and lovers,
and all the profound characters
from her favourite fantasies
tried their fate
to open that lock.

Some brought different kinds
of special keys;
some took years
to forge master keys.
Some dedicated their entire lives
to become the keymaker
who could pick that lock.

All of them
tried one by one, and failed.

But they were not ready
to accept such failure,
so they gathered,
joined hands,
and called a blacksmith.

The blacksmith brought a hammer
and began to strike it down.

The lock did not budge,
but the heart started to bleed.
It began with a few drops,
and soon started
to bleed profusely.

Then came a voice through the door:
Stop it.
Stop it.
Stop it.

It was my voice.

The gathering was dazed.
Who was this being
who had trespassed the gates?
How could someone own the heart
they had all been trying to win?

Envy arose among them,
and they ordered the blacksmith
to continue the hammering.

My voice came again:
I have the key.
I have the key.
I have the key.

But you do not need it.

'Why?'
they screamed in unison.

And I responded:

'You fools.
You are already residents of her heart,
and the door,
the door you are trying to break into,

is locked from inside.

And I,
despite having the key,
am not allowed in.'

SALT

You do not read all the poems
that I write.
Some of them are made of water
and taste salty.
They pour down from my eyes,
and like the rest of my poems,
they too are about you.

Laughing Stock

My love,
sometimes I am a laughing stock
for the people around me,
for the intensity of the love
I have for you,
already knowing
that it has a very bleak
chance of being reciprocated.

They think
they have learned it all
about love,
its beginning,
its development,
its course,
and its very end.

These people take everything
in life as a game,
and while living only
by the concept of triumph,
they warn me about the game of love
and how I am going to lose it.

Sometimes,
they make me picture
self-abasing myself
as a lonely old man,
lashing his drooping skin
with his own hands,
beating his chest

for the foolishness
he committed years ago;

as an old man
living in a madhouse,
relentlessly gurgling your name,
chanting absurd love songs
in the hope of your arrival;

as an old man
having lost everything to love,
the sense of time,
and the sense of self;

as an old man
carrying a magnifying glass
and looking for certain patterns
from the gods of fate
in stones and abstractions
that would assure your love for me.

And while they do this,
my heart oscillates
between fire and fire,
thorns and thorns,
abyss and abyss,
both afraid to collapse
and suffering the swing.

Then I pretend to be
the character
they want to see me in.
I laugh along with them,
louder than their guffaws,
already beating my chest

and performing joy
in their callous jokes.

But amid all this,
I pity them.
I pity them
for their artlessness.
I pity them
for their rational brains
that are too coward
to lose anything.

I pity them for believing
that love is only whole
when it is possessed.

Renaissance

All the masterpieces created until today,
Paintings,
Sculptures,
works of literature,
pieces of music,
and the rest of the greatest artworks,
if they were animated
and bestowed with consciousness,
a heart,
and the same aesthetic sense as human beings,
then I would want all of them
to meet you once,

so they would know
that if you were to be transformed
into some kind of art,
then the Renaissance
must start with you.

A Thousand Moons

You once said to me
that you are not beautiful.
I looked into your eyes
and stayed silent.

I did not say a word,
because you were right.

You were right because,
since the first time I had seen you
and known you,
I had understood
that the thing called 'beauty'
would have to wear
a thousand moons over its skin
to become a fraction
of what you are.

PROMISE

And I promise you,
none of my sperm
is ever going to form a life,
if it does not meet
any egg of yours.

BEFORE BEING A LOVER

Before being a lover,
I want to be a mother to you,
and a father,
and a brother,
and a sister,
and a best friend,
and all those people
who have ever loved you
more than themselves,

because my love,
when it comes to you,
I become so selfish
that I wish to carry
all the love within me
that you will ever need.

One

The pieces of me
long for the pieces of you,
as if we were a single soul
and a single body
in some other lifetime.

MISTAKEN

You are mistaken to believe
that I do not have you.
You are all that my lungs breathe.
My skin shimmers
with the fire of your eyes,
and my bones are ingrained
with the caress of your hands.

I am recomposed
of all the little pieces
you left in me.

And, my love,
I swear to you,
in my body
we are knit together
in such a way that,
when I die,
I will burst forth
with the fragrance
you were born with.

Embrace

I do not have a clue
about how long I will hug you
when we meet,
but I swear to our love,
I will hold you there,
in my arms,
enclosed and locked,
for hours and hours,

until our chests align
to the rhythm of our breathing,
until our hands forget
who they belong to,
until you begin to feel
that your bones are
wearing my skin,
and two of our bodies
have become one,
until our body scents
have given birth
to a third fragrance.

And, my love,
if you allow me,
I can hold you like that,
in my arms,
enclosed and locked,
for the rest of our lives.

Loneliness

Someone asked me
how I could be lonely
when I have a family,
friends,
and a purpose to live.

I have everything
except you,
and that does not make me alone.

And I tell them
this loneliness is
the loneliness of my soul,
my soul that has been traveling
from an endless time
towards you,
towards itself,
seeking nothing but you.

And this loneliness will stay
until my soul reaches
its destination,
until it reaches you,
until it reaches itself,
until it becomes itself,
until it becomes whole,
until it becomes one,
and then explodes.

INKING

If I could ink one poem
upon your heart forever,
it would talk about the love
that I have for you,
and how it is deeper than
the love of those
who brought you into this life,
and deeper than
the love of those
with whom you have spent
your longest time.

It would talk about
the fire of your beauty
and its blinding spell upon me,
from which a thousand sorcerers
could not liberate me.

It would talk about
how I could save this world
with your hand in mine,
about the adventures,
all forms of art,
and the countless memories
I am yet to make with you,
and how all of this
is one of the main reasons
I am still alive.

In the end,
it would talk about
the atoms you are

and the atoms I am,
and how the atoms I am
will remain pointless
and meaningless
until they merge into
the atoms you are.

Orange Umbrella

It was raining,
and she needed her orange umbrella,
but she would not ask the umbrella to save her,
because she believed that the umbrella,
like every time, would understand.

But the umbrella was too far
to know it was raining,
let alone understand her.

There were many umbrellas around,
in different colors and aromas,
waiting to save her
and dying to be held,
but our girl wanted only the orange one,
for a secret reason.

The secret reason
was the color and shape
of her old scars,
which were orange too.

So she kept getting drenched,
and a terrible thought crossed her mind
as the drizzle turned into a rainstorm.
She thought she would let the rain punish her
for wanting that umbrella.

But all of a sudden,
it stopped raining.

She smiled to herself,
wondering how she had tricked the rain
into sympathizing with her.

But just then,
one more raindrop
fell on her nose.

Little did she know
that it was the sky
who had been weeping
for not being
the orange umbrella.

Oneness

Every time you are away from me,
your body carries
two souls,
two minds,
and two hearts,

and all I am left with
is a frame
of bones and flesh,
searching for,
but not wanting,
its interiors back.

Bathing

One day
this universe may go cold,
but even then
my atoms
will be bathing in the fire
of your love.

FIRE

I am never going to believe
that you are not fire
until your skin touches mine
and leaves it
without being inflamed.

Presence

I do not know my own composition,
but what I know is that
without you,
I turn empty,
become parched,
and grow barren.

And in your presence,
I can lend
a thousand oceans
to the Earth.

Eyes

Your eyes have a way
with my heart;
they beat through it
as if it looks through them.

BHARATA

My wife dies often,
sometimes once a week,
and at times once a fortnight.
There are just two of us
in a big house
in a small village,
and we do not talk to anyone else,
except for a black man
with a foot-long ponytail.
And for some strange reason,
all the villagers loathe us.

So, all alone,
I have to carry her body
over my shoulders
to the crematorium,
and, as part of the routine,
I read her a poem on the way.

And please know
the most important part:
as I read her the poem,
and if she finds it good enough,
her body starts to move
and she resurrects,
and we head back home together,
while I carry her
over my shoulders.

But if she does not like the poem,
she remains motionless and dies,
and her cremation takes place.

Before I tell you more,
you need to know
how we got married.
It is the kind of story
that is remembered
and talked about
for many generations.
It is also my go-to story
for all the strangers in me
whom I meet every night
in my dreams.

It was summer
the first time we met
in a group,
in a restaurant.
We were a bunch of monsters together,
most of us in our early twenties.
I hardly noticed her,
except that she carried
her small backpack
over her chest
instead of her back,
and wore sleeves
over her arms
to avoid tanning.

I was smitten
the second time we met,
and I still can not figure out
why or how,
but somehow,
she fell for me too.

Fast forward ten years:
we got married
and had four babies,
three girls
and a boy.
The part I have skipped in between
is reserved
for one of my books,
which is yet to be written.

This morning,
she died,
and I carried her
over my shoulders
and walked
toward the crematorium.
And as part of the routine,
I began to recite her a new poem
about how I would end up
if we were not together.
I told her
I would do things
the dark would not handle,
and the light would refuse
to stand behind.

Sadly, she did not like the poem,
because I reached the crematorium
and her body did not move even a little.

'Has she passed away this time?'
asked the black man
with the foot-long ponytail,
who was in charge

of the crematorium.

'Yes,' I was wailing.

'Please cremate her fast.
I am late, and I have to take
a new bag of wood stock and clay home.'
My crying grew louder.

Like always, he understood,
and she was cremated.

Somewhere in the same village,
a mother was scolding
her young son
for not studying.

'You will end up
like Bharata,
the madman.
Like him,
you will keep reciting poetry
to yourself
and end up never getting married,
only to become a sculptor.
Like him,
you will make statues
of your imaginary wife
and cremate them
every now and then.
And when you actually
flunk your exams
and completely turn
into Bharata,
please burn yourself

along with the statue
of your wife.

STUDY!
You dog,
this time will never return!'

TRUTH

I want you to wear my soul,
and flare my bones,
and breathe my skin,
and read my smell,
and touch my voice,
and listen to my silence,
and drink my name,
and question my pain.

I want you to take me
to those places within me
where I fear going alone,
and to those places
that only you can see,
and to those places
that are yet to be discovered.

I want you to peel me off,
layer by layer,
until I am left with the gist
that controls the art I am.

And when you do that,
I promise you,
I will become the truth
you are searching for.

UNAWARE

At this moment,
it is impossible for me
to fathom what you pine for,
but it will be the greatest tragedy
of my life
if you surrender to some mountain
in awe of its heights,
or give in to some ocean
out of curiosity for its vastness.

Because, my love,
all you have learned about my fire
is that it can merely light
a few sticks,
while I have kept you unaware
of all those parts
that could blind the sun one day.

Sword

Even if you were a sword,
I would have held you by the hilt
and pressed your tip against my lips.

And if you demanded to cut something,
I would have offered you my flesh
to play with.

And if you needed to sharpen yourself,
I would have let you work
on my bare bones.

And to keep you safe,
I would have made
my chest
a sheath.

MAGIC

Sometimes,
I think of the moment
when you would have pictured us together,
despite all the fences
and the silence between us;
when you dared to disrupt
all the shackles around you
and within you;
when you let your soul
spring over your heart,
passing over decoying roads
and pulling through the sharpest thorns,
all for the sake of
one beautiful possibility,
that I,
only I,
know the magic
that can save you.

INSUFFICIENT

On most days,
I'm not enough even for myself,
and wanting you
becomes a sin
that every cell inside me
commits.

DRESSING

I will tear my own skin apart
and present its shreds to you
as dressing
for every single wound
this world has given you.

Night Like That

My love,
I imagine a night
where you are lying with me,
resting your head on my arm,
and your hand over my chest,
while I stroke your back
until you fall asleep,
slowly drifting into dreams,
and I watch you sleeping
and dreaming until dawn,
until you wake up,
and I think to myself
how,
just how,
I could be so fortunate to have you,
to be able to take care of you,
to be with you,
beside you
while being alive,

and for a night like that
I can trade my entire life.

Entity

I have spent night after night
looking for similes and metaphors
that would precisely define your entity.

I have contemplated oceans, air,
the moon, fire, goddesses, and the sun,
but nothing conforms to what you are,
from abstractions to manifestations,
from words to phrases,
and from truth to fiction;
language, art, and philosophy,
everything has failed me.

Maybe you just can not be described,
like the meaning of life,
holding the greatest quest of the human race
in its miraculous wonders.

Describe My Love

If I were to narrate my love for you,
I would not use pompous words
to romanticize the truth.
I would not even speak.

I would simply become a hush.

But despite such silence,
the unspoken words of my love
would still reach you,
from my soul to your soul,
from the energy I am
to the energy you are,

like nectar appears in a flower,
and a heartbeat appears in an embryo,
through those spiritual miracles of life
that can never be deciphered by humans.

PUKE

My mother made a joke
about my love for you,
as to how
I am besotted with you.
She said to me
that I would even drink your puke.

I stayed silent for a while.

And then I leaned closer
and whispered into her ears
that I would drink it
without a second thought,
if I had to.

Because of that whisper,
and the silence between,
she had understood
that I meant my words.

Separation

This separation,
it is not a mere break
you have taken
to make us work
upon our individualities.

It is a death
that takes birth inside me
every morning,
and I keep hollering your name
the whole day
inside my head,
and into the crater of our separation

Beloved,
I have not come to Earth
to win accolades or laurels,
or to etch my name
onto the keystones of human history.

I am the mystery
that was created for you,
which you are going to solve
every day
and every night
until the end of my existence.

MUSE

Not a single poem
that reaches you
is written by me.

All these shards,
if you ask me the truth,
are plucked by you,
through me,
from me.

It is I
who am the muse,
and you
who are the poet.

Bunch of Words

I am a bunch of words
that have been thrown
into the space around you,
which only you can put into order.

Entirely surrendered,
these words are waiting
for your mystic hands
to bind them together.

And you,
my poetess,
you will hold these words,
one by one,
and build me
from worthless
sagging shards
into a piece of art.

And even if you form
a tragedy,
let it be so beautiful
that everyone
who reads it
would dream of being
the poem it becomes
or the poetess
that you are.

Only Poem

You are the only poem
I want to write,
every day
and every night,
until the rest of my life,
over and over again.

Words Know Nothing

I am relentlessly looking for
the words
to make you feel
everything I feel.

With those words,
I try to lay a path
from my mind to your mind,
from my heart to your heart,
and from my soul to your soul,

but words
and language
do not suffice.

Words are misunderstood.
Language is misunderstood.
Love is lost in words.
Truth is lost in language.

So give me your wounds,
and I will become a remedy.
Give me your heart,
and my heart will build
a home with it,
Give me your skin,
and my skin will write
masterpieces on it.

Surrender yourself to me.
I will surrender myself to you.

And only then you will discover
that the same words,
which preach love
know nothing about it.

DESTINATION

You once asked me
what was different
that I saw in you,
and honestly,
I did not have a real answer.

My love for you
has been unreasonable
right from the beginning,
like something
that is simply meant to be,
something I have
no choice
or control over.

I could write
a thousand poems
to tell you how
and why I love you,
but all of them
would be based
on my imagination
of what I think
of you and us.

But the truth is,
I still do not have
a real answer.

And maybe,
half of my soul
lies in your body,

and half of your soul
lies in my body,
and both these halves
are yearning
to return
to their real destination.

Lethal Art

My love,
there is a reason
people do not get along with you
for too long.

You are made up of raw feelings,
cruel poetry,
grave music,
rad paintings,
and all that is art,

and such art is lethal.
It is like a clean mirror
that reveals people
to their true selves,

their flaws,
their timidity,
and their ignorance
toward innate desires
and passions
they have buried somewhere
and forgotten.

You strip them
of their worldly skins,
and their facades
that make them feel secure.
You strip them
of their conformity.

They would not tell you,
but it is difficult
to be stripped of something
they have acquired over the years
in the name of experience.
And it is difficult to handle
such nudity
in this pragmatic world.

So they begin
to distance themselves from you.

But do not let any departure
weaken you,
because among those people
there would be a few quiet watchers
who would understand your language,
and listen to
the symphony of your soul,
and silently believe in you.

And maybe,
there is someone out there,
someone equally exhausted,
someone who sheds the same tears,
someone made up of you,
who is dying to get naked
along with you,
at the brink of your arrival.

TOGETHER

Until we are together,
you will find me lost
and swaying
between
the thoughts and ideas
of the things
I want to do with you,
and the things
I want to do to you.

LIPS

Even if your lips were soaked in poison,
I would suck them dry
and turn them into a question
that only my lips can answer.

INADEQUATE

There are as many flowers
inside my chest
that you could make a chain
to wrap the moon
infinite times over,
and still they fall short
to let you know
how special you are.

Part of Me

There is a part of me,
which I have been hiding and saving my whole life,
and that part is only meant for you to see.

It is a part
far more sacred than any shrine,
far more beautiful than the full moon,
and far more precious than any art or stone,
and I can not explain it to you
with words,
or any kind of art,
or my silence.

I can not hand it to you
like a thanksgiving or birthday present.
You could explore my entire body
and still would not find it.

But when we are together,
measuring the roads with our ride,
dancing to sad and happy songs,
discussing our flaws
and the injustice done to us,
drinking the poison and beauty of this life,
creating meaning out of this chaos,
standing strong amid the forces
trying to break us apart,

in one of those moments
you will feel that part,
like a bare soul
being touched for the first time,

and the touch pulsating its truth,
leaving the soul content
and trembling.

Perhaps in that moment,
you will throw yourself into my arms
and start to weep,
and I will weep too,
holding us together,
against the world,

against the gods,
against the universe.

And I promise you,
if we are never together,
and I am not able to show that part to you,
it will remain within me,
hidden and protected
until the rest of my life,
and cremated along with my body.

Poem of the Universe

This universe is writing
a love poem for us,
that began
when one could hold the universe
in the palm of hands,
and will end
when the universe no longer evolves.

We,
my love,
are the muses of this universe,
a poet
who, I think,
will commit suicide
if we do not end up together.

Making Love

I want to make love to you
to the point where
all the tiny pores of your skin
reek of my smell,
and your neck
grows into a transverse flute
that I go on playing
as I pull your hair back,
and your lips are eaten with fervor,
unable to distinguish between
your tongue and mine,
and my hands reaching
each part of you
make you unlearn all the fears,
and your thighs no longer tremble
at the sound of love,
and your lungs
are filled with my breath,
and your bones ache sweetly
wanting more of me,
and your back,
which you once thought was fragile,
braves all my waves
crashing into you,
and your feet learn
that they are as hungry as your breasts,
and your body feels light as a leaf
vanishing into my skies,
and your eyes
marvel and master
the language of power and surrender.

I want to make love to you
as if I am purging your body
by fixing it with mine.
I want to make love to you
by becoming a potter to your earth
and carving you into all those shapes
that you never thought were possible.

I want to make love to you
like animals make love,
devoid of any shame,
and as hard as it gets.

I want to make love to you
as I write my poems,
ruthlessly
and mindfully.

Holding Your Hands

Just holding your hands
would flood the caves
of my heart,
and I can never imagine
where your kiss would leave me.

PICTURE

The day we get married
this universe will
take its first picture.

Silent Promise

There is a silent
promise between you and me,
a promise thicker than a thousand vows,
the kind of promise
there are no words for,
one that only we can understand.

Please keep that promise,
and I swear to you,
I will bring all the gods
back to earth
to cry for us.

GLORY

Maybe
this universe was incarnated
to witness
the glory
of our love.

ONE DAY

One day,
you will cry,
burying your head
in my chest,
and ask me
why,
why I love you this much.

And to answer that,
I will push you a little farther
and metamorphose myself
into a mirror,
the kind of mirror
that can look through souls.

Growing Old Without You

If I grow old without you,
then I can imagine myself like this,
on some random night,
in some corner of the world,
in a dark, dense room,
with my lungs brimmed with smoke
and my chest-length beard
reeking of cigarette butts,
with a shitload of alcohol
lurching through my guts.

I am writing poems to you,
for you,
which you will never read.

In your absence,
pain sits beside me to read those poems,
sharing the drags
and clinking her goblet with mine.
She and I,
we make a nice couple.

I start to understand her,
and she,
unlike you,
starts to understand me too.

In those throbbing months and years,
trembling through random nights,
listening to our raw story
and marveling at my madness for you,
she,

unlike you,
names herself after me
and claims the crown
meant for you.

Until one night,
finally,
she grumbles to me,
as to why
I never write for her,
but only you.

So I,
like you,
choose silence this time,
for I know
even if I married her,
but I still
love you more.

Arrival and Departure

Love arrives like a fire,
a fire with a face,
a face with a certain oneness in it,
as if it is the face
you have known for centuries,
for countless births,
and from a time when you did not exist,
as if it is the face
you are to recognize in this life,
as if it is the face
you were meant to squish
and play with,
as if it is the face
that is going to wear
all the laughter,
all the suffering,
emerging from
and breaking into your life.

Love arrives like a fire,
a fire,
with a voice
that hollers at you,
jump,
jump, jump,
and you are scared,
scared of the flames,
scorches, burns,
and of the strange aftermaths,
so you do not jump.
You just stand there,
looking at the love,

trying to calculate the incalculable,
the size of its truth,
the potency of its flames,
the stretch of its promise.

And slowly,
after months and years,

after you have marveled at
and relished everything
that love could offer
from a distance,
it begins to change its shape.

The fire with a face and a voice
slowly turns into a silent kite,
which you have been flying
since the arrival of love,
and if you are still brave enough
to examine the kite,
you will discover
your own voice echoing through it,
and your own face written all over it.

And on a random day,
the kite breaks away from your hands,
carrying more of you
than your remains
trying to hold onto it,
and that is how love departs,
like a broken kite
with unknown destination,
which you can
no longer see,
but are riding on.

God of Love

If I were the God of love,
I would rob love from all matter.
I would rob the stars of the love in their light,
rob the planets of the love in their chaotic forms,
rob black holes of the love they swallow from around them,
rob the universe of the love driving its incessant evolution.

I would rob tiny cells of the love in their nuclei,
rob leaves and trees of the love they breathe in and breathe out,
rob every living thing of the love that sustains it.

I would rob lifeless things of their love as well,
rob air and fire,
rob stones and rocks of the love in their silence,
rob rivers and oceans of the love in their silent screams.

I would rob the whole of human history of love,
rob the love waiting in the future.
I would rob religions, prayers, literature,
I would rob every word ever written
or yet to be written of love,
and finally, I would rob love of itself.

If I were the God of love,
I would hold all that robbed love upon my lips,
all of it,
all of it yearning to be exhausted
in a single moment,
only to kiss your feet.

PROOF

I will love you in ways
nobody has ever been loved before.
I will love you in ways
nobody will ever be loved after,
and there is no analogy
for that kind of love.

I,
my love,
will be the
living or dead proof
in the faces of gods,
making them change
their answer with my name
whenever questioned about love.

Lessons

If you want to quench
the thirst of my soul,
then please do not turn into water,
for my soul is wild,
wild,
wild like fire.
And this fire seeks fire.

So when you come to me,
please come to me as fire,
and together
we will burn into each other.

And I promise you
that our burning
will teach the gods of love
as to how
to make love.

Marry

If I could have it my way,
I would marry you every day,
over and over again,
until the day
I die,

and then
I would marry you from my grave,
with my tombstone
making you
the promises of forever
and its words
kissing your lips.

Golden Truths

My love,
once you told me
you had popped far too many sleeping pills,
and it was a miracle that you survived.
It was a suicide attempt.

And after that,
my perspective about you changed.
I began to see you as a blue flower
that takes a new birth every morning,
and it should not be spoken loudly,
let alone about sensitive things.

I framed my words carefully
in each of our conversations.
I never told you
about my own suffering;
while you were a flower that was blue,
a certain darkness had turned me
into a blade that was red, meant to cut,
meant to hurt.
And there was no way
a blue flower could find a home in a red blade.

Another time, you told me
you could not feel love for anyone,
neither men nor women,
and your life was nothing
but a dry black river,
and only the art flowing through it
was its savior.

I was scared,
like a poet on his deathbed,
scared, having written you
thousands of words immersed in love,
and how those words would have hurt you,
when each of them begged for your love,
because I had known
that not being able to return love
is also a suffering of its own kind.

Now that you are caged in
some part of the world,
I want to confess something.
I want you to know
a poet on his deathbed
just drank from the dry black river,
and the blue flower has found
a home in the red blade.

And you,
who could have been in the arms of God,
chose a cage
that you thought would
promise freedom.

Own You

Yes,
I want to own you,
all of you,
all for me,
just for me.

And when I say this,
I also want you to understand,
that I am not a cage,
but another universe
that wants you,
only you,
to open itself to.

TESTIFYING

A thousand miles apart,
the amount of love
that I derive from you,
none of your lovers could derive
a fraction of it,
even in your presence.

Nobody could make enough love
to the entire universe of your body
that I can make
to a single atom of it.

No one
in this multiverse
loves you
as much as I do,
and the warmth reaching your heart
through the continuous burning
of the soul that I am
will go on testifying to this.

Infinite Odysseys

My love,
have we not known each other
long before this life,
long before the countless lives,
long before the existence of existence,
when we were nothing,
and when we created ourselves from nothing,
when we created the gods,
and procreated time,
and taught the gods about
the magic of creation,

My love,
have we not known each other
long before this life,
long before the countless lives,
and when we failed
to discover the truth of existence,
so we made the gods
create this universe
inside the multiverse we had created,
and made them turn us into cells
by passing all our powers to them,
only to seek the truth as creations
that we could not discover as creators.

My love,
have we not known each other
long before this life,
the lives,
when we struggled through infinite odysseys,
from being cells

to all the forms of animals,
from vertebrates to mammals
that have ever existed,
and the lives as humans,
when we hunted together,
to the early civilizations,
when we carved stone with our nails,
to the dark ages,
when we were mugged by our own creations,
to the Renaissance,
when we painted pseudo-gods,
to this life.

My love,
have we not known each other,
long before this life,
long before the countless lives,
long before the existence of existence,
when, with my strength,
I could bend the multiverse to its toes,
to this life,
when I am writing these silly lines
to make you recognize me,
and when I am too fragile
to endure the suffering of existence.

My love,
it was not in vain,
everything we have been through.
I may have found the truth.
Where are you?

Forgotten

How could you forget my lips,
those tiny parts of my anatomy,
those messengers of truth,
those bridges to the abyss of my fire?

For ages and ages,
for countless lives,
they have danced upon yours,
beneath yours,
inside yours,
and made you taste the earth in me.

It's not their curves,
their fragrance,
their color,
or even their movement
that I am asking you to remember.

I am talking about the existential hunger,
the hunger of the soul
that gorges on itself,
about the quest for meaning
in the futility of existence,
about your ever burgeoning loneliness
in spaces unknown to you.

These lips of mine
could end it all.

Irreplaceable

I could find,
melt,
and win
the heart of God,
but then,
even God can not replace you.

Insignificant Part

My last words for you
will be written on my tombstone;
they will talk about the life
you lived inside me,
and how my own life
was just an insignificant
part of it.

Dust

In the end,
everything is dust,
all of us,
and true or not,
let us blindly believe
that the dust we become
will carry the memories
of how hard we loved,
and how
we all were once
a collection
of live embers
burning in
and burning for love.

Perpetual Poem

I want to be buried with you,
in one grave,
we upon each other,
our bodies resting forever
in the womb of the earth,
and our souls
in the peace of eternity,
and in a love beyond it.

And let our tombstone read:
here lies
a perpetual love poem
writing itself.

From My Nothingness

I love you today,
and I will love you tomorrow,
and the day after that,
and the day after that,
until I am alive.

I will love you forever,
and I will love you beyond forever,
if such forever is limited
to our lifetimes.

I will love you
beyond all dimensions of time.
I will love you even after I die,
from my ashes and my remains,
for they will carry
my love for you,
either beneath the earth
or in space,
buried or floating.

I will love you
from the stardust I become.
I will love you
until this universe
kisses the apocalypse,
and I will love you
after that too,
from my nothingness.

AUTHOR'S NOTE:

If you are reading this book between 2026 and 2030, and centralized global governance rooted in Civitology has still not been adopted, I want to confess something.

I believe art is what makes life meaningful. However, given the way human civilization is evolving and converging, our children may no longer be able to create, enjoy, or cherish art. We are moving toward an ecological and structural collapse from which there may be no return.

The most effective way to restore ecosystems, mitigate climate change to 1.5 degrees Celsius, maintain peace, and sustain human civilization on Earth for the next 10,000 years is to enact centralized global governance rooted in Civitology, replace capitalism with Civitalism, and unite all national armies into a single world army. Without adopting this path, the collapse of human civilization within the coming years becomes inevitable. The longer we delay adopting this path, the closer we move to the collapse.

You may wonder how you can contribute. One way is to write letters and emails to the global elite and world leaders, and to protest peacefully for this cause. Another way is to hold these same actors accountable and openly shame them for robbing the future of our children and their own children, merely to preserve and abuse regional power in the name of sovereignty. I leave that choice to you.

We are here for a brief moment. I hope we do the best we can to protect the future of humanity. I hope you read my other book, *Civitology: The Science of Civilizational Longevity*, and understand that what I am talking about is not just important, but essential to our collective survival.

If any part of this poetry collection stays with you, let it move beyond these pages. Photograph a poem you connect with and tag me on Instagram, pin a piece, share it with someone who may need it, or write a review or email me your thoughts. If you feel this book belongs with another reader, recommend it. The farther it travels, the more suffering it may reduce.

www.ingramcontent.com/pod-product-compliance
Lightning Source LLC
Chambersburg PA
CBHW062142160726
48282CB00027B/906
* 9 7 8 9 3 3 4 3 0 9 9 2 8 *